Non-Executive Directors

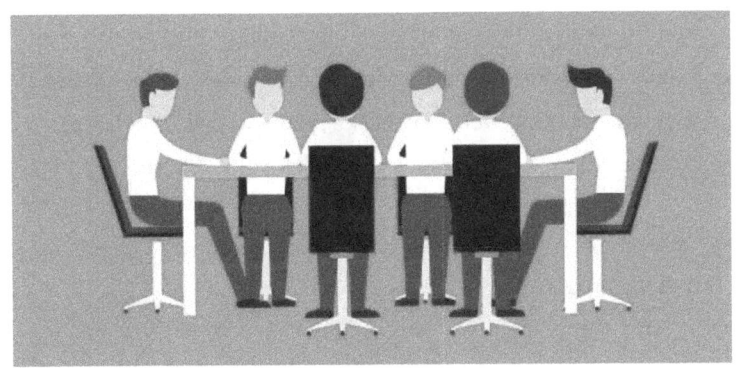

What they are and how to become one.

By Ray Fox

First Edition published in 2017 by The Bottom Line Consultancy

Hurst Cottage, Bottle Square Lane, Radnage,

Buckinghamshire. HP14 4DP, United Kingdom

Tel: 01494 483728 Fax: 01494 484039

Email: fox@estelle-alan.com

Ray Fox has asserted his right to be identified as the author of this work in accordance with sections 77 and 78 of the Copyright, Designs and Patents Act 1988.

ISBN-13: 978-1982023553
ISBN-10: 1982023554

First edition 2017

Printed and bound by Amazon Creates

NOTE: The material contained in this book is set out in good faith for general guidance and no liability can be accepted for loss or expense incurred as a result of relying in particular circumstances on statements made in this book. Laws and regulations are complex and liable to change, and readers should check the current positions with the relevant authorities in their country of origin before making personal arrangements.

This book is available online and at all good bookstores.

Contents

Introduction

In 1994, I was the Company Secretary and Legal Director of a US$3B turnover American Corporation. For reasons that aren't important here, I decided to strike out on my own.

One of the areas of business that interested me was to become a Non-Executive Director. To be honest, I didn't really know that much about Non-Executive Directors other than the fact that they seemed to charge what to me seemed a phenomenal amount of money to attend board meetings.

I first came across Non-Executive Directors about thirty years ago when I was working for Dun & Bradstreet, one of the world's biggest business information companies.

We had a Non-Executive Director on our board. He was a politician, a former member of Ted Heath's cabinet. It took me quite a while to work out why he was on our board as he said very little at board meetings. However, he was incredibly effective and impressive whenever we had important visitors and sales prospects from overseas. He was regularly asked to entertain them at The Houses of Parliament, lunch on the terrace, a private tour of the Commons and the Lords, etc.

The point here is that we're all unique, we all have diverse skill sets and we all have something distinctive to offer different companies.

I recently came across a sarcastic comment made by Ken Morrison, the former Chairman of Morrisons Supermarkets – he asked "what's the difference between a Non-Executive Director and a supermarket trolley?" The answer – "you can usually get more booze into a Non-Executive Director than a supermarket trolley."

So much for his perception – but what's the reality?

What is a Non-Executive Director?

Interestingly enough, there is no legal definition for a Non-Executive Director, so let's start with what a Director is.

When a company is formed, the founders of the company are known as Subscribers. These Subscribers come together to agree to set up a company and they become the first shareholders. In order to get the company off the ground, they sign what is known as a Memorandum of Association.

At the same time as the Memorandum of Association is signed, Articles of Association are prepared. The Articles of Association basically set out how the company should be run.

A draft set of Memorandum and Articles of Association are shown in Appendix 1.

The first shareholders then appoint the first Directors of the Company. In most companies, the first Directors who are appointed are usually the first shareholders, but this isn't always the case.

The Directors are appointed to manage the day-to-day business activities and finances and to ensure all statutory filing obligations are met. Directors must act lawfully and honestly and make decisions for the benefit of the company and its members. Using their skills, experience and judgment, Directors must try to make the company a success by promoting and achieving its business objectives.

The Duties and Responsibilities

The duties and responsibilities of a company Director are set out in the various Companies Acts, the Articles of Association and any service contract that is put in place between a Director and the firm. The Companies Acts outline a statutory regime for Directors' duties, which consists of seven principle requirements:

1. To act within the powers granted to them in the Articles of Association.

2. To promote the success of the business.

3. To exercise independent judgement in all decision-making.

4. To use reasonable care, skill and diligence at all times.

5. To avoid or declare any conflict of interest.

6. To avoid the acceptance of benefits from third parties or using their position to make private profits.

7. To declare an interest in a proposed transaction or arrangement with the company before it enters into such a transaction.

For the majority of companies, the directors are full time employees of the company and work exclusively for that company.   They are sometimes known as Executive Directors.

A Non-Executive Director is a member of the board of Directors of a company or organisation who does not form part of the employed executive management team. They are not employees of the company and are differentiated from Directors who are members of the board who also have executive responsibilities. However they do have the same legal duties, responsibilities and potential liabilities as their executive counterparts.

Fundamentally, the Non-Executive Director role is to provide a creative contribution and improvement to the board by providing dispassionate and objective criticism. Their role may change depending on the organisation, though they are usually not involved in the day-to-day management of the company but monitor the executive activity and contribute to the development strategy.

How are Non-Executive Directors normally found and appointed?

Many years ago, by pure chance, [I was approached by a friend of a friend of a friend] I became a Non-Executive Director of a small private company. I loved it. I found that holding a Non-Executive Directorship can have many benefits. Certainly, the additional income was attractive. Perhaps, more importantly, it led to job satisfaction, an increased level of networking and contacts, job security, a sense of worth and contribution plus a feeling that I was doing something good and that it was appreciated. Do you get this in your current employment?

After that experience, I found that I wanted more Non-Executive Director appointments. Perhaps you do as well, or possibly you are looking to become a Non-Executive Director for the first time.

I started researching the market place with two simple questions – "How do I promote myself to obtain Non-Executive Director appointments?" and "What can I offer organisations that would be of interest to them?" Quite simply, I hit a brick wall!! What I found was that the market place was 100% geared to companies finding people but there was nothing that helped people find companies.

I seemed to have come across a glass ceiling. I kept reading in the business press that So-and-So had been appointed as a Director of Harry Bloggings PLC but I couldn't work out how he or she had got that appointment.

It seemed that the market place was driven by companies who had identified that they had a need for a Non-Executive Director and then went out into the market place to find one.

Generally, they did one of two things.

Option one, as Chris Tarrant would say, was "phone a friend". To use common parlance, they relied on "the old boys' network". They would approach someone they knew from the Rotary, the Business Link, the Masons, the golf club, their church group, etc and offer them the opportunity. They might not necessarily be the right person, but at least there were no costs involved in their recruitment and the problem was quickly solved.

From the perspective of someone like you and me who are looking for Non-Executive Directorship opportunities, this is really quite galling. Previously, there would have been a company looking for a Non-Executive Director for which you might have had the ideal qualifications and experience, yet you didn't even know the position was available.

Option two, would be for them to approach a recruitment or headhunting consultancy. The problem with this option is that it incurs a charge of anything between £10,000 and £15,000 so this is not a particularly attractive option for the Company. Again the difficulty from your perspective is that you then have to trawl through all the national newspapers, submit your CV to hundreds of recruitment consultants and hope that your CV and experience match the Clients' requirements.

The whole process is haphazard and from my perspective, completely reactive. There was no way that I could find out about an opportunity before it came on the market.

The NED Exchange

That's where the idea for my Company, The NED Exchange [www.NEDexchange.co.uk] was born.

Over the years, we've had literally hundreds and hundreds of organizations approach us looking for Non-Executive Directors.

They range from the bizarre, to the peculiar and to the more usual. As examples, we have been asked to find Non-Executive Directors who were Russian speaking experts in the international phosphorus market, an economist who had experience of the Syrian Agricultural industry, a Non-Executive Director who had previously been a Director of a Premiership Football Club, someone with experience of high street Italian retail furniture, the funeral director industry, experience of the swimwear market, the dental industry, the opticians industry, etc.

At the time of writing this book, we have organisations looking for someone with experience of Taekwondo, running a museum, educational trusts, a Port

Authority, a charitable organisation for children's health care, a University Students Union, a law firm in Scotland, the General Lighthouse Authority in Scotland, a privately owned business providing outsourced funding solutions, a Governmental Board in Northern Ireland, a Trust that provides supported housing to people with mental ill health, a Financial Services organisation in the Channel Islands, an SME manufacturer of automotive components, an East London charity, the governing body for British Snow Sports, an investment company, a multi-academy trust of three secondary schools and a social housing provider.

Something that all prospective Non-Executive Directors should consider is that just as there are Non-Executive Directors looking for organisations, there are organisations looking for Non-Executive Directors.

So why would anyone want to become a Non-Executive Director?

Most people think it's for the money. Certainly an additional income is a major incentive for many people but how much should you charge?

I treat a Non-Executive Director appointment in the same way that I would treat a consulting assignment. I personally charge £2,000 a day for the consulting work that I do although I have to say that some of my business associates think I'm a cheap skate as they charge £3,000 or even £3,500 a day.

Just imagine that you were asking Richard Branson or Alan Sugar to be on your board – who knows what they would charge? Maybe £5,000 a day – perhaps more. Regardless of your political views, how much would Tony Blair, David Cameron or George Osborne charge?

On the other hand, most commercial Non-Executive Director appointments are for one day a month for three years – equivalent to thirty six days at £2,000 a day which equals £72,000 over three years.

Having said that, I regularly get enquiries from organisations looking for a Non-Executive Director but they can only offer, say, £250 a day. I always tell them that you invariably get what you pay for and that if you want Arfer Daley or Dell Boy, then £250 a day sounds about right.

However, you must remember that some individuals are NOT looking for a daily fee. Some prospective Non-Executive Directors are retired and are happy to "give back" in an altruistic fashion. Others are looking to invest money. Others are happy investing "sweat equity" – they will work for free and take equity in the company at some time in the future, especially should the company float.

You also have to consider what the organisation is looking for.

Many of them have a short term skill shortage and are looking for someone to come in and plug the gap.

Others have a specific project that they are looking at and need someone to come in with that particular experience.

For example, they might be relocating, launching a new product range, starting to export into a specific country for the first time, they might be floating, introducing a social media policy, etc.

Sometimes, they just might need someone with grey hairs and wisdom, someone who has the right contacts and/or someone who understands a balance sheet, a profit and loss account and knows what an aged debt analysis is!

To give you an example, many years ago I was a Non-Executive Director on the board of a property development company. They had a phenomenal opportunity to purchase a block of land at a discount and needed to borrow £20M at short notice.

By coincidence, I had a business colleague who was the Vice President of a major bank who I knew were interested in lending to property developers.

Within twenty four hours, I had arranged a meeting between the bank VP and the Directors of the property development company.

A couple of weeks later, the deal was concluded and the bank even paid me £5,000 commission as a finders' fee. Not bad for a fifteen minute phone call!

What type of person is suited to this role?

Ambitious business professionals have tremendous advantages when they come to consider applying for and accepting Non-Executive Director appointments.

Business professionals have a unique insight into the governance and compliance of running a company and are invariably comfortable with the boardroom discussions.

Effective Non-Executive Directors should be able to challenge the perceived views and opinions of their executive colleagues, to debate constructively and rigorously challenge the view of "this is the way we've always done things."

You must be prepared to bring a calm and reasoned voice to board meetings where, on occasions, tempers are frayed and voices are raised.

Your experience of being able to weigh up the facts as you see them, to be able to present them in a calm demeanour in the face of, perhaps, hostile individuals protecting their commercial territory and sometimes their integrity, makes you a unique asset.

Sometimes you'll need to hold your ground when challenged, present sound judgment and a strength of character – perhaps skill sets that you possess but don't get an opportunity to exercise in your full time employment.

It's important that you understand that Non-Executive Directors must emphasise the long term needs of the organisation and leave aside any petty squabbles or personal differences.

Your function as a Non-Executive Director is not to micro manage the way the organisation runs but to take an overview whereby you can protect the organisation's reputation as well as its future growth and survival. You are, in essence, a facilitator to support and encourage the board.

No matter what organisation you act for as a Non-Executive Director, and no matter what personal skills you actually have, a Non-Executive Director has to understand that along with the rest of the board, they are responsible for the finance and stewardship of the organisation's assets.

How do I find Non-Executive Director opportunities?

There are no short cuts to finding Non-Executive Director opportunities. However, the way the market has changed with the growth of the internet, an increasing number of opportunities are promoted online.

In appendix 2, I have listed a number of the more popular websites that promote Non-Executive Director opportunities.

What is the Tax situation?

HMRC's starting point is that Non-Executive Directors should be treated in the same way as executive directors for PAYE purposes. This is because both executive and Non-Executive Directors are regarded as office holders. There is no statutory definition of the word 'office' but it has been judicially defined as a:

"permanent, substantive position which had an existence independent from the person who filled it, which went on and was filled in succession by successive holders." [Rowlatt J in Great Western Railway Company v Bater 8TC231.]

As an office holder, these individuals are taxed in relation to their director fees. Payments falling under these provisions are subject to PAYE and NIC via the payroll.

HMRC does not accept that it is possible for Non-Executive Directors to carry out their office holder duties in a self-employed capacity. However, a Non-Executive Director may also provide consultancy services to the same company and it is the nature of the consultancy arrangement which determines its tax and NIC treatment.

In the past, a practice has grown of Non-Executive Directors invoicing for their services via a personal service company (PSC). The Non-Executive Directors may receive, via the PSC, fees from several unrelated companies with which he or she holds offices. Historically, many held the view that such fees could be paid gross to the PSC but HMRC has never subscribed to this view.

My advice would be to talk to an accountant to ensure that you pay the appropriate tax and national insurance.

What's next?

I would recommend that you have a proper letter of appointment agreed between yourself and the

Company appointing you. I have prepared a draft in Appendix 3 but you should seek professional legal advice to ensure that you are properly protected.

A Word of Warning

There are many organisations in the UK market place who will tell you that they will help you find Non-Executive Director opportunities. You need to be cautious with your time and careful with your money. Many of these organisations just organise networking events and run training courses to tell you how to become Non-Executive Directors. I'm sure that they have value and a place in the market.

However, just be careful you don't end up spending thousands of pounds just to be told that you need to submit your cv to head-hunters and recruitment firms and register with online agencies.

Certainly you need to be active in submitting your cv and applying for opportunities. We've been running The NED Exchange for well over twenty years and we have an extraordinarily high year-on-year renewal rate. Obviously, some of our members don't renew. When I speak to them, by far the majority of those who don't renew have never applied for any of the hundreds and hundreds of Non-Executive Director opportunities that we generate. You are also able to place a summary of your cv on our website, which is a totally free service.

In other words, I would recommend that you get active in applying for opportunities rather than spend thousands of pounds going on a training course.

Appendix 1

MEMORANDUM AND ARTICLES OF ASSOCIATION OF
(NAME) LIMITED ('COMPANY')

MEMORANDUM OF ASSOCIATION OF
(NAME) LIMITED

The Companies Act 2006

COMPANY LIMITED BY SHARES

Each subscriber to this memorandum of association wishes to form a company under the Companies Act 2006 and agrees to become a member of the Company and to take at least one share.

Name of subscriber: Authentication by subscriber:

....

....

....

....
(name)   *(signature)*

Date:.................................

SCHEDULE 1 REGULATION 2

MODEL ARTICLES FOR PRIVATE COMPANIES LIMITED BY SHARES

INDEX TO THE ARTICLES

PART 1 – INTERPRETATION AND LIMITATION OF LIABILITY

PART 2 – DIRECTORS' POWERS AND RESPONSIBILITIES

Decision-making by directors

Appointment of directors

PART 3 – SHARES AND DISTRIBUTIONS

Shares

Dividends and other distributions

Capitalisation of profits

PART 4 – DECISION-MAKING BY SHAREHOLDERS

Organisation of general meetings

PART 1 – INTERPRETATION AND LIMITATION OF LIABILITY

Defined terms

1. In the articles, unless the context requires otherwise:

- "articles" means the company's articles of association
- "bankruptcy" includes individual insolvency proceedings in a jurisdiction other than England and Wales or Northern Ireland

which have an effect similar to that of bankruptcy

- "chairman" has the meaning given in article 12
- "chairman of the meeting" has the meaning given in article 39
- "Companies Acts" means the Companies Acts (as defined in section 2 of the Companies Act 2006), in so far as they apply to the company
- "director" means a director of the company, and includes any person occupying the position of director, by whatever name called
- "distribution recipient" has the meaning given in article 31
- "document" includes, unless otherwise specified, any document sent or supplied in electronic form
- "electronic form" has the meaning given in section 1168 of the Companies Act 2006
- "fully paid" in relation to a share, means that the nominal value and any premium to be paid to the company in respect of that share have been paid to the company
- "hard copy form" has the meaning given in section 1168 of the Companies Act 2006
- "holder" in relation to shares means the person whose name is entered in the register of members as the holder of the shares
- "instrument" means a document in hard copy form
- "ordinary resolution" has the meaning given in section 282 of the Companies Act 2006
- "paid" means paid or credited as paid
- "participate", in relation to a directors' meeting, has the meaning given in article 10
- "proxy notice" has the meaning given in article 45
- "shareholder" means a person who is the holder of a share
- "shares" means shares in the company
- "special resolution" has the meaning given in section 283 of the Companies Act 2006

- "subsidiary" has the meaning given in section 1159 of the Companies Act 2006
- "transmittee" means a person entitled to a share by reason of the death or bankruptcy of a shareholder or otherwise by operation of law; and
- "writing" means the representation or reproduction of words, symbols or other information in a visible form by any method or combination of methods, whether sent or supplied in electronic form or otherwise.

Unless the context otherwise requires, other words or expressions contained in these articles bear the same meaning as in the Companies Act 2006 as in force on the date when these articles become binding on the company.

Liability of members

2. The liability of the members is limited to the amount, if any, unpaid on the shares held by them.

PART 2 – DIRECTORS' POWERS AND RESPONSIBILITIES

Directors' general authority

3. Subject to the articles, the directors are responsible for the management of the company's business, for which purpose they may exercise all the powers of the company.

Shareholders' reserve power

4. (1) The shareholders may, by special resolution, direct the directors to take, or refrain from taking, specified action.
   (2) No such special resolution invalidates anything which the directors have done before the passing of the resolution.

Directors may delegate

5. (1) Subject to the articles, the directors may delegate any of the powers which are conferred on them under the articles:

    (a) to such person or committee
    (b) by such means (including by power of attorney)
    (c) to such an extent
    (d) in relation to such matters or territories; and
    (e) on such terms and conditions

    as they think fit.

    (2) If the directors so specify, any such delegation may authorise further delegation of the directors' powers by any person to whom they are delegated.

    (3) The directors may revoke any delegation in whole or part, or alter its terms and conditions.

Committees

6. (1) Committees to which the directors delegate any of their powers must follow procedures which are based as far as they are applicable on those provisions of the articles which govern the taking of decisions by directors.

    (2) The directors may make rules of procedure for all or any committees, which prevail over rules derived from the articles if they are not consistent with them.

DECISION-MAKING BY DIRECTORS

Directors to take decisions collectively

7. (1) The general rule about decision-making by directors is that any

decision of the directors must be either a majority decision at a meeting or a decision taken in accordance with article 8.

(2) If:

(a) the company only has one director, and

(b) no provision of the articles requires it to have more than one director, the general rule does not apply, and the director may take decisions without regard to any of the provisions of the articles relating to directors' decision-making.

Unanimous decisions

8. (1) A decision of the directors is taken in accordance with this article when all eligible directors indicate to each other by any means that they share a common view on a matter.

(2) Such a decision may take the form of a resolution in writing, copies of which have been signed by each eligible director or to which each eligible director has otherwise indicated agreement in writing.

(3) References in this article to eligible directors are to directors who would have been entitled to vote on the matter had it been proposed as a resolution at a directors' meeting.

(4) A decision may not be taken in accordance with this article if the eligible directors would not have formed a quorum at such a meeting.

Calling a directors' meeting

9. (1) Any director may call a directors' meeting by giving notice of the meeting to the directors or by authorising the company secretary (if any) to give such notice.

(2) Notice of any directors' meeting must indicate:

    (a) its proposed date and time
    (b) where it is to take place; and
    (c) if it is anticipated that directors participating in the meeting will not be in the same place, how it is proposed that they should communicate with each other during the meeting.

(3) Notice of a directors' meeting must be given to each director, but need not be in writing.

(4) Notice of a directors' meeting need not be given to directors who waive their entitlement to notice of that meeting, by giving notice to that effect to the company not more than seven days after the date on which the meeting is held. Where such notice is given after the meeting has been held, that does not affect the validity of the meeting, or of any business conducted at it.

Participation in directors' meetings

10. (1) Subject to the articles, directors participate in a directors' meeting, or part of a directors' meeting, when:

    (a) the meeting has been called and takes place in accordance with the articles, and
    (b) they can each communicate to the others any information or opinions they have on any particular item of the business of the meeting.

(2) In determining whether directors are participating in a directors' meeting, it is irrelevant where any director is or how they communicate with each other.

(3) If all the directors participating in a meeting are not in the same place, they may decide that the meeting is to be treated as taking place wherever any of them is.

Quorum for directors' meetings

11. (1) At a directors' meeting, unless a quorum is participating, no proposal is to be voted on, except a proposal to call another meeting.

    (2) The quorum for directors' meetings may be fixed from time to time by a decision of the directors, but it must never be less than two, and unless otherwise fixed it is two.

    (3) If the total number of directors for the time being is less than the quorum required, the directors must not take any decision other than a decision:

      (a) to appoint further directors, or
      (b) to call a general meeting so as to enable the shareholders to appoint further directors.

Chairing of directors' meetings

12. (1) The directors may appoint a director to chair their meetings.

    (2) The person so appointed for the time being is known as the chairman.

    (3) The directors may terminate the chairman's appointment at any time.

    (4) If the chairman is not participating in a directors' meeting within ten minutes of the time at which it was to start, the participating directors must appoint one of themselves to chair it.

Casting vote

13. (1) If the numbers of votes for and against a proposal are equal, the chairman or other director chairing the meeting has a casting vote.

    (2) But this does not apply if, in accordance with the articles, the chairman or other director is not to be counted as participating in the decision-making process for quorum or voting purposes.

Conflicts of interest

14. (1) If a proposed decision of the directors is concerned with an actual or proposed transaction or arrangement with the company in which a director is interested, that director is not to be counted as participating in the decision-making process for quorum or voting purposes.

(2) But if paragraph (3) applies, a director who is interested in an actual or proposed transaction or arrangement with the company is to be counted as participating in the decision-making process for quorum and voting purposes.

(3) This paragraph applies when:

  (a) the company by ordinary resolution disapplies the provision of the articles which would otherwise prevent a director from being counted as participating in the decision-making process

  (b) the director's interest cannot reasonably be regarded as likely to give rise to a conflict of interest; or

  (c) the director's conflict of interest arises from a permitted cause.

(4) For the purposes of this article, the following are permitted causes:

  (a) a guarantee given, or to be given, by or to a director in respect of an obligation incurred by or on behalf of the company or any of its subsidiaries

  (b) subscription, or an agreement to subscribe, for shares or other securities of the company or any of its subsidiaries, or to underwrite, sub-underwrite, or guarantee subscription for any such shares or securities; and

  (c) arrangements pursuant to which benefits are made available to employees and directors or former employees and directors of the company or any of its subsidiaries which do not provide special benefits for directors or former directors.

(5) For the purposes of this article, references to proposed decisions and decision-making processes include any directors' meeting or part of a directors' meeting.

(6) Subject to paragraph (7), if a question arises at a meeting of directors or of a committee of directors as to the right of a director to participate in the meeting (or part of the meeting) for voting or quorum purposes, the question may, before the conclusion of the meeting, be referred to the chairman whose ruling in relation to any director other than the chairman is to be final and conclusive.

(7) If any question as to the right to participate in the meeting (or part of the meeting) should arise in respect of the chairman, the question is to be decided by a decision of the directors at that meeting, for which purpose the chairman is not to be counted as participating in the meeting (or that part of the meeting) for voting or quorum purposes.

Records of decisions to be kept

15. The directors must ensure that the company keeps a record, in writing, for at least ten years from the date of the decision recorded, of every unanimous or majority decision taken by the directors.

Directors' discretion to make further rules

16. Subject to the articles, the directors may make any rule which they think fit about how they take decisions, and about how such rules are to be recorded or communicated to directors.

APPOINTMENT OF DIRECTORS

Methods of appointing directors

17. (1) Any person who is willing to act as a director, and is permitted by law to do so, may be appointed to be a director:

(a) by ordinary resolution, or

(b) by a decision of the directors.

(2) In any case where, as a result of death, the company has no shareholders and no directors, the personal representatives of the last shareholder to have died have the right, by notice in writing, to appoint a person to be a director.

(3) For the purposes of paragraph (2), where two or more shareholders die in circumstances rendering it uncertain who was the last to die, a younger shareholder is deemed to have survived an older shareholder.

Termination of director's appointment

18. A person ceases to be a director as soon as:

(a) that person ceases to be a director by virtue of any provision of the Companies Act 2006 or is prohibited from being a director by law

(b) a bankruptcy order is made against that person

(c) a composition is made with that person's creditors generally in satisfaction of that person's debts

(d) a registered medical practitioner who is treating that person gives a written opinion to the company stating that that person has become physically or mentally incapable of acting as a director and may remain so for more than three months

(e) notification is received by the company from the director that the director is resigning from office, and such resignation has taken effect in accordance with its terms.

Directors' remuneration

19. (1) Directors may undertake any services for the company that the directors decide.

(2) Directors are entitled to such remuneration as the directors determine:

(a) for their services to the company as directors, and
(b) for any other service which they undertake for the company.

(3) Subject to the articles, a director's remuneration may:

(a) take any form, and
(b) include any arrangements in connection with the payment of a pension, allowance or gratuity, or any death, sickness or disability benefits, to or in respect of that director.

(4) Unless the directors decide otherwise, directors' remuneration accrues from day to day.

(5) Unless the directors decide otherwise, directors are not accountable to the company for any remuneration which they receive as directors or other officers or employees of the company's subsidiaries or of any other body corporate in which the company is interested.

Directors' expenses

20. The company may pay any reasonable expenses which the directors properly incur in connection with their attendance at:

(a) meetings of directors or committees of directors
(b) general meetings, or
(c) separate meetings of the holders of any class of shares or of debentures of the company, or otherwise in connection with the exercise of their powers and the discharge of their responsibilities in relation to the company.

PART 3 – SHARES AND DISTRIBUTIONS

SHARES

All shares to be fully paid up

21. (1) No share is to be issued for less than the aggregate of its nominal value and any premium to be paid to the company in consideration for its issue.

    (2) This does not apply to shares taken on the formation of the company by the subscribers to the company's memorandum.

Powers to issue different classes of share

22. (1) Subject to the articles, but without prejudice to the rights attached to any existing share, the company may issue shares with such rights or restrictions as may be determined by ordinary resolution.

    (2) The company may issue shares which are to be redeemed, or are liable to be redeemed at the option of the company or the holder, and the directors may determine the terms, conditions and manner of redemption of any such shares.

Company not bound by less than absolute interests

23. Except as required by law, no person is to be recognised by the company as holding any share upon any trust, and except as otherwise required by law or the articles, the company is not in any way to be bound by or recognise any interest in a share other than the holder's absolute ownership of it and all the rights attaching to it.

Share certificates

24. (1) The company must issue each shareholder, free of charge, with one or more certificates in respect of the shares which that shareholder holds.

    (2) Every certificate must specify:

    (a) in respect of how many shares, of what class, it is issued
    (b) the nominal value of those shares
    (c) that the shares are fully paid; and
    (d) any distinguishing numbers assigned to them.

    (3) No certificate may be issued in respect of shares of more than one class.

    (4) If more than one person holds a share, only one certificate may be issued in respect of it.

    (5) Certificates must:

    (a) have affixed to them the company's common seal, or
    (b) be otherwise executed in accordance with the Companies Acts.

Replacement share certificates

25. (1) If a certificate issued in respect of a shareholder's shares is:

    (a) damaged or defaced, or
    (b) said to be lost, stolen or destroyed, that shareholder is entitled to be issued with a replacement certificate in respect of the same shares.

    (2) A shareholder exercising the right to be issued with such a replacement certificate:

    (a) may at the same time exercise the right to be issued with a single certificate or separate certificates

    (b) must return the certificate which is to be replaced to the company if it is damaged or defaced; and

    (c) must comply with such conditions as to evidence, indemnity and the payment of a reasonable fee as the directors decide.

Share transfers

26. (1) Shares may be transferred by means of an instrument of transfer in any usual form or any other form approved by the directors, which is executed by or on behalf of the transferor.

    (2) No fee may be charged for registering any instrument of transfer or other document relating to or affecting the title to any share.

    (3) The company may retain any instrument of transfer which is registered.

    (4) The transferor remains the holder of a share until the transferee's name is entered in the register of members as holder of it.

    (5) The directors may refuse to register the transfer of a share, and if they do so, the instrument of transfer must be returned to the transferee with the notice of refusal unless they suspect that the proposed transfer may be fraudulent.

Transmission of shares

27. (1) If title to a share passes to a transmittee, the company may only recognise the transmittee as having any title to that share.

    (2) A transmittee who produces such evidence of entitlement to shares as the directors may properly require:

(a) may, subject to the articles, choose either to become the holder of those shares or to have them transferred to another person, and

(b) subject to the articles, and pending any transfer of the shares to another person, has the same rights as the holder had.

(3) *But transmittees do not have the right to attend or vote at a general meeting, or agree to a proposed written resolution, in respect of shares to which they are entitled, by reason of the holder's death or bankruptcy or otherwise, unless they become the holders of those shares.*

Exercise of transmittees' rights

28. (1) Transmittees who wish to become the holders of shares to which they have become entitled must notify the company in writing of that wish.

(2) If the transmittee wishes to have a share transferred to another person, the transmittee must execute an instrument of transfer in respect of it.

(3) Any transfer made or executed under this article is to be treated as if it were made or executed by the person from whom the transmittee has derived rights in respect of the share, and as if the event which gave rise to the transmission had not occurred.

Transmittees bound by prior notices

29. If a notice is given to a shareholder in respect of shares and a transmittee is entitled to those shares, the transmittee is bound by the notice if it was given to the shareholder before the transmittee's name has been entered in the register of members.

DIVIDENDS AND OTHER DISTRIBUTIONS

Procedure for declaring dividends

30. (1) The company may by ordinary resolution declare dividends, and the directors may decide to pay interim dividends.

(2) A dividend must not be declared unless the directors have made a recommendation as to its amount. Such a dividend must not exceed the amount recommended by the directors.

(3) No dividend may be declared or paid unless it is in accordance with shareholders' respective rights.

(4) Unless the shareholders' resolution to declare or directors' decision to pay a dividend, or the terms on which shares are issued, specify otherwise, it must be paid by reference to each shareholder's holding of shares on the date of the resolution or decision to declare or pay it.

(5) If the company's share capital is divided into different classes, no interim dividend may be paid on shares carrying deferred or non-preferred rights if, at the time of payment, any preferential dividend is in arrear.

(6) The directors may pay at intervals any dividend payable at a fixed rate if it appears to them that the profits available for distribution justify the payment.

(7) If the directors act in good faith, they do not incur any liability to the holders of shares conferring preferred rights for any loss they may suffer by the lawful payment of an interim dividend on shares with deferred or non-preferred rights.

Payment of dividends and other distributions

31. (1) Where a dividend or other sum which is a distribution is payable in respect of a share, it must be paid by one or more of the

following means:

(a) transfer to a bank or building society account specified by the distribution recipient either in writing or as the directors may otherwise decide

(b) sending a cheque made payable to the distribution recipient by post to the distribution recipient at the distribution recipient's registered address (if the distribution recipient is a holder of the share), or (in any other case) to an address specified by the distribution recipient either in writing or as the directors may otherwise decide

(c) sending a cheque made payable to such person by post to such person at such address as the distribution recipient has specified either in writing or as the directors may otherwise decide; or

(d) any other means of payment as the directors agree with the distribution recipient either in writing or by such other means as the directors decide.

(2) In the articles, "the distribution recipient" means, in respect of a share in respect of which a dividend or other sum is payable:

(a) the holder of the share; or

(b) if the share has two or more joint holders, whichever of them is named first in the register of members; or

(c) if the holder is no longer entitled to the share by reason of death or bankruptcy, or otherwise by operation of law, the transmittee.

No interest on distributions

32. The company may not pay interest on any dividend or other sum payable in respect of a share unless otherwise provided by:

(a) the terms on which the share was issued, or

(b) the provisions of another agreement between the holder of that share and the company.

Unclaimed distributions

33. (1) All dividends or other sums which are:

    (a) payable in respect of shares, and

    (b) unclaimed after having been declared or become payable,

    may be invested or otherwise made use of by the directors for the benefit of the company until claimed.

  (2) The payment of any such dividend or other sum into a separate account does not make the company a trustee in respect of it.

  (3) If:

    (a) twelve years have passed from the date on which a dividend or other sum became due for payment, and

    (b) the distribution recipient has not claimed it, the distribution recipient is no longer entitled to that dividend or other sum and it ceases to remain owing by the company.

Non-cash distributions

34. (1) Subject to the terms of issue of the share in question, the company may, by ordinary resolution on the recommendation of the directors, decide to pay all or part of a dividend or other distribution payable in respect of a share by transferring non-cash assets of equivalent value (including, without limitation, shares or other securities in any company).

  (2) For the purposes of paying a non-cash distribution, the directors may make whatever arrangements they think fit, including, where any difficulty arises regarding the distribution:

    (a) fixing the value of any assets

    (b) paying cash to any distribution recipient on the basis of that value in order to adjust the rights of recipients; and

(c) vesting any assets in trustees.

Waiver of distributions

35. Distribution recipients may waive their entitlement to a dividend or other distribution payable in respect of a share by giving the company notice in writing to that effect, but if:

   (a) the share has more than one holder, or
   (b) more than one person is entitled to the share, whether by reason of the death or bankruptcy of one or more joint holders, or otherwise, the notice is not effective unless it is expressed to be given, and signed, by all the holders or persons otherwise entitled to the share.

CAPITALISATION OF PROFITS

Authority to capitalise and appropriation of capitalised sums

36. (1) Subject to the articles, the directors may, if they are so authorised by an ordinary resolution:

   (a) decide to capitalise any profits of the company (whether or not they are available for distribution) which are not required for paying a preferential dividend, or any sum standing to the credit of the company's share premium account or capital redemption reserve; and
   (b) appropriate any sum which they so decide to capitalise (a "capitalised sum") to the persons who would have been entitled to it if it were distributed by way of dividend (the "persons entitled") and in the same proportions.

(2) Capitalised sums must be applied:

   (a) on behalf of the persons entitled, and

53

(b) in the same proportions as a dividend would have been distributed to them.

(3) Any capitalised sum may be applied in paying up new shares of a nominal amount equal to the capitalised sum which are then allotted credited as fully paid to the persons entitled or as they may direct.

(4) A capitalised sum which was appropriated from profits available for distribution may be applied in paying up new debentures of the company which are then allotted credited as fully paid to the persons entitled or as they may direct.

(5) Subject to the articles the directors may:

(a) apply capitalised sums in accordance with paragraphs (3) and (4) partly in one way and partly in another

(b) make such arrangements as they think fit to deal with shares or debentures becoming distributable in fractions under this article (including the issuing of fractional certificates or the making of cash payments); and

c) authorise any person to enter into an agreement with the company on behalf of all the persons entitled which is binding on them in respect of the allotment of shares and debentures to them under this article.

PART 4 – DECISION MAKING BY SHAREHOLDERS

ORGANISATION OF GENERAL MEETINGS

Attendance and speaking at general meetings

37. (1) A person is able to exercise the right to speak at a general meeting when that person is in a position to communicate to all those attending the meeting, during the meeting, any

information or opinions which that person has on the business of the meeting.

(2) A person is able to exercise the right to vote at a general meeting when:

   (a) that person is able to vote, during the meeting, on resolutions put to the vote at the meeting, and
   (b) that person's vote can be taken into account in determining whether or not such resolutions are passed at the same time as the votes of all the other persons attending the meeting.

(3) The directors may make whatever arrangements they consider appropriate to enable those attending a general meeting to exercise their rights to speak or vote at it.

(4) In determining attendance at a general meeting, it is immaterial whether any two or more members attending it are in the same place as each other.

(5) Two or more persons who are not in the same place as each other attend a general meeting if their circumstances are such that if they have (or were to have) rights to speak and vote at that meeting, they are (or would be) able to exercise them.

Quorum for general meetings

38. No business other than the appointment of the chairman of the meeting is to be transacted at a general meeting if the persons attending it do not constitute a quorum.

Chairing general meetings

39. (1) If the directors have appointed a chairman, the chairman shall chair general meetings if present and willing to do so.

(2) If the directors have not appointed a chairman, or if the chairman is unwilling to chair the meeting or is not present within ten minutes of the time at which a meeting was due to start:

(a) the directors present, or

(b) (if no directors are present), the meeting, must appoint a director or shareholder to chair the meeting, and the appointment of the chairman of the meeting must be the first business of the meeting.

(3) The person chairing a meeting in accordance with this article is referred to as "the chairman of the meeting".

Attendance and speaking by directors and non-shareholders

40. (1) Directors may attend and speak at general meetings, whether or not they are shareholders.

(2) The chairman of the meeting may permit other persons who are not:

(a) shareholders of the company, or

(b) otherwise entitled to exercise the rights of shareholders in relation to general meetings, to attend and speak at a general meeting.

Adjournment

41. (1) If the persons attending a general meeting within half an hour of the time at which the meeting was due to start do not constitute a quorum, or if during a meeting a quorum ceases to be present, the chairman of the meeting must adjourn it.

(2) The chairman of the meeting may adjourn a general meeting at which a quorum is present if:

(a) the meeting consents to an adjournment, or

(b) it appears to the chairman of the meeting that an adjournment is necessary to protect the safety of any person attending the meeting or ensure that the business of the meeting is conducted in an orderly manner.

(3) The chairman of the meeting must adjourn a general meeting if directed to do so by the meeting.

(4) When adjourning a general meeting, the chairman of the meeting must

(a) either specify the time and place to which it is adjourned or state that it is to continue at a time and place to be fixed by the directors, and

(b) have regard to any directions as to the time and place of any adjournment which have been given by the meeting.

(5) If the continuation of an adjourned meeting is to take place more than 14 days after it was adjourned, the company must give at least 7 clear days' notice of it (that is, excluding the day of the adjourned meeting and the day on which the notice is given):

(a) to the same persons to whom notice of the company's general meetings is required to be given, and

(b) containing the same information which such notice is required to contain.

(6) No business may be transacted at an adjourned general meeting which could not properly have been transacted at the meeting if the adjournment had not taken place.

VOTING AT GENERAL MEETINGS

Voting: general

42. A resolution put to the vote of a general meeting must be decided on a show of hands unless a poll is duly demanded in accordance with the articles.

Errors and disputes

43. (1) No objection may be raised to the qualification of any person voting at a general meeting except at the meeting or adjourned meeting at which the vote objected to is tendered, and every vote not disallowed at the meeting is valid.

   (2) Any such objection must be referred to the chairman of the meeting, whose decision is final.

Poll votes

44. (1) A poll on a resolution may be demanded:

   (a) in advance of the general meeting where it is to be put to the vote, or
   (b) at a general meeting, either before a show of hands on that resolution or immediately after the result of a show of hands on that resolution is declared.

   (2) A poll may be demanded by:

   (a) the chairman of the meeting
   (b) the directors
   (c) two or more persons having the right to vote on the resolution; or
   (d) a person or persons representing not less than one tenth of the total voting rights of all the shareholders having the

right to vote on the resolution.

(3) A demand for a poll may be withdrawn if:

    (a) the poll has not yet been taken, and
    (b) the chairman of the meeting consents to the withdrawal.

(4) Polls must be taken immediately and in such manner as the chairman of the meeting directs.

Content of proxy notices

45. (1) Proxies may only validly be appointed by a notice in writing (a "proxy notice") which:

    (a) states the name and address of the shareholder appointing the proxy
    (b) identifies the person appointed to be that shareholder's proxy and the general meeting in relation to which that person is appointed
    (c) is signed by or on behalf of the shareholder appointing the proxy, or is authenticated in such manner as the directors may determine; and
    (d) is delivered to the company in accordance with the articles and any instructions contained in the notice of the general meeting to which they relate.

(2) The company may require proxy notices to be delivered in a particular form, and may specify different forms for different purposes.

(3) Proxy notices may specify how the proxy appointed under them is to vote (or that the proxy is to abstain from voting) on one or more resolutions.

(4) Unless a proxy notice indicates otherwise, it must be treated as:

(a) allowing the person appointed under it as a proxy discretion as to how to vote on any ancillary or procedural resolutions put to the meeting, and

(b) appointing that person as a proxy in relation to any adjournment of the general meeting to which it relates as well as the meeting itself.

Delivery of proxy notices

46. (1) A person who is entitled to attend, speak or vote (either on a show of hands or on a poll) at a general meeting remains so entitled in respect of that meeting or any adjournment of it, even though a valid proxy notice has been delivered to the company by or on behalf of that person.

(2) An appointment under a proxy notice may be revoked by delivering to the company a notice in writing given by or on behalf of the person by whom or on whose behalf the proxy notice was given.

(3) A notice revoking a proxy appointment only takes effect if it is delivered before the start of the meeting or adjourned meeting to which it relates.

(4) If a proxy notice is not executed by the person appointing the proxy, it must be accompanied by written evidence of the authority of the person who executed it to execute it on the appointor's behalf.

Amendments to resolutions

47. (1) An ordinary resolution to be proposed at a general meeting may be amended by ordinary resolution if:

(a) notice of the proposed amendment is given to the company in writing by a person entitled to vote at the general meeting at which it is to be proposed not less than 48 hours before the meeting is to take place (or such later time as the chairman of the meeting may determine), and

(b) the proposed amendment does not, in the reasonable opinion of the chairman of the meeting, materially alter the scope of the resolution.

(2) A special resolution to be proposed at a general meeting may be amended by ordinary resolution, if:

(a) the chairman of the meeting proposes the amendment at the general meeting at which the resolution is to be proposed, and

(b) the amendment does not go beyond what is necessary to correct a grammatical or other non-substantive error in the resolution.

(3) If the chairman of the meeting, acting in good faith, wrongly decides that an amendment to a resolution is out of order, the chairman's error does not invalidate the vote on that resolution.

PART 5 – ADMINISTRATIVE ARRANGEMENTS

Means of communication to be used

48. (1) Subject to the articles, anything sent or supplied by or to the company under the articles may be sent or supplied in any way in which the Companies Act 2006 provides for documents or information which are authorised or required by any provision of that Act to be sent or supplied by or to the company.

(2) Subject to the articles, any notice or document to be sent or supplied to a director in connection with the taking of decisions by directors may also be sent or supplied by the means by

which that director has asked to be sent or supplied with such notices or documents for the time being.

(3) A director may agree with the company that notices or documents sent to that director in a particular way are to be deemed to have been received within a specified time of their being sent, and for the specified time to be less than 48 hours.

Company seals

49. (1) Any common seal may only be used by the authority of the directors.

(2) The directors may decide by what means and in what form any common seal is to be used.

(3) Unless otherwise decided by the directors, if the company has a common seal and it is affixed to a document, the document must also be signed by at least one authorised person in the presence of a witness who attests the signature.

(4) For the purposes of this article, an authorised person is:

(a) any director of the company
(b) the company secretary (if any); or
(c) any person authorised by the directors for the purpose of signing documents to which the common seal is applied.

No right to inspect accounts and other records

50. Except as provided by law or authorised by the directors or an ordinary resolution of the company, no person is entitled to inspect any of the company's accounting or other records or documents merely by virtue of being a shareholder.

Provision for employees on cessation of business

51. The directors may decide to make provision for the benefit of persons employed or formerly employed by the company or any of its subsidiaries (other than a director or former director or shadow director) in connection with the cessation or transfer to any person of the whole or part of the undertaking of the company or that subsidiary.

DIRECTORS' INDEMNITY AND INSURANCE

Indemnity

52. (1) Subject to paragraph (2), a relevant director of the company or an associated company may be indemnified out of the company's assets against:

(a) any liability incurred by that director in connection with any negligence, default, breach of duty or breach of trust in relation to the company or an associated company

(b) any liability incurred by that director in connection with the activities of the company or an associated company in its capacity as a trustee of an occupational pension scheme (as defined in section 235(6) of the Companies Act 2006)

(c) any other liability incurred by that director as an officer of the company or an associated company.

(2) This article does not authorise any Indemnity which would be prohibited or rendered void by any provision of the Companies Acts or by any other provision of law.

(3) In this article:

(a) companies are associated if one is a subsidiary of the other or both are subsidiaries of the same body corporate, and

(b) a "relevant director" means any director or former director

63

of the company or an associated company.

Insurance

53. (1) The directors may decide to purchase and maintain insurance, at the expense of the company, for the benefit of any relevant director in respect of any relevant loss.

(2) In this article:

(a) a "relevant director" means any director or former director of the company or an associated company

(b) a "relevant loss" means any loss or liability which has been or may be incurred by a relevant director in connection with that director's duties or powers in relation to the company, any associated company or any pension fund or employees' share scheme of the company or associated company, and

(c) companies are associated if one is a subsidiary of the other or both are subsidiaries of the same body corporate.

Appendix 2

LIST OF ONLINE RESOURCES

http://www.careersinrecruitment.com/jobs?keyword=Non+Executive+Director

http://appointments.thesundaytimes.co.uk/jobs

http://ukvacancycentral.co.uk

http://appointments.thesundaytimes.co.uk/searchjobs/?Keywords=Non+Executive+Director&radialtown=&LocationId=&RadialLocation=5

http://appointments.thesundaytimes.co.uk/jobs/non-executive-director/

http://www.resonatesearch.co.uk/all-current-positions

http://www.beyond-recruitment.co.uk/Candidate/Vacancy/searchvacancy.aspx

http://www.sugarjobs.co.uk

http://jobs.economist.com/

http://www.moonconsulting.co.uk

http://www.delni.gov.uk/
http://www.jobsonline.co.uk/

http://jobs.theguardian.com/

http://www.jobs.ac.uk/

http://jobs.telegraph.co.uk/

http://www.drdni.gov.uk/

http://applications.appointed-for-scotland.org/

http://jobs.scotsman.com/

http://www.indeed.co.uk/

http://www.nijobfinder.co.uk/

http://www.jobswales.co.uk/

http://wales.gov.uk/?lang=en

http://publicappointments.cabinetoffice.gov.uk/applications/s
earch

http://nonexecdirector.co.uk/candidates/available-roles

http://publicappointments.cabinetoffice.gov.uk/

http://www.publicjobsdirect.com

http://www.appointed-for-scotland.org/

http://www.strike-jobs.co.uk

http://www.greatjobsinteaching.co.uk/

http://www.careerbuilder.co.uk/

http://www.simplyhired.co.uk

http://www.reed.co.uk/employment

http://www.michaelpage.co.uk

http://www.njobs.org.uk/

http://www.wig.co.uk/home

http://www.adzuna.co.uk/

http://www.nonexecutivedirector.co.uk/roles-non-executive-director.asp

http://nonexecutives-unlimited.co.uk/currentvacancies.html

http://www.gatenbysanderson.com/results/?job_type=All&keywords=Non,Executive,director

http://www.monster.co.uk/

http://www.fish4.co.uk/

http://www.jobsite.co.uk/

http://www.exec2exec.com/

http://www.icaewjobs.com/

http://jobs.dailymail.co.uk/

http://www.careersandjobsuk.com/

http://www.publicappointmentsni.org/

http://www.executivesontheweb.com/

http://www.exec-appointments.com/

http://www.matureaccountants.com/vacancies3.php

http://www.cv-library.co.uk

http://www.civvyjobs.com/

http://www.hanoverfox.com/search/

http://www.jobstoday.co.uk/

http://www.charityjob.co.uk

http://www.ntda.nhs.uk/

http://www.professionalpensionsjobs.com/

http://www.careervolunteer.co.uk/roles

http://www.nonexecutivedirectors.com/ned-vacancies.php

http://www.novoexec.com

http://www.davidsonpartners.com

http://www.totaljobs.com

http://www.jobs.co.uk

http://www.wickland-westcott.co.uk/current-positions/

https://russam-gms.co.uk

http://www.sercanto.co.uk/

http://www.russellreynolds.com/executive-opportunities/search

http://www.jobsgopublic.com

http://www.jobheaven.co.uk

http://www.ukstaffsearch.com

http://www.venturexec.com

http://www.networxrecruitment.com/website/jobseekers

http://www.adderleyfeatherstone.com

http://www.barnabystewart.com/candidates

http://www.myjobscotland.gov.uk

http://www.hinde-smith.com/vacancies.aspx

http://candidates.capabilityjane.com/

http://www.orbit.org.uk/careers/vacancies/

http://keystone.jobs/

http://jobs.trovit.co.uk/

http://www.nidirect.gov.uk/public-appointment-vacancies

http://uk.jobrapido.com

http://www.executive-i.com/executiveJobs.htm

http://attenti.co.uk

http://www.s1jobs.com

http://www.searchukjobs.com

http://www.efinancialcareers.co.uk

http://www.allen-york.com

http://jobs.salusdigital.co.uk/job-search-results/Non+Executive+director/oo-kw

http://www.onlinejobhunt.co.uk

http://www.london4jobs.co.uk

http://www.cityjobs.com

http://www.ivyexec.com

Appendix 3

DRAFT NON-EXECUTIVE DIRECTOR LETTER OF APPOINTMENT

Dear Joe Blow

In this Letter of Agreement, the following definitions apply:

Articles of Association	The Articles of Association of the Company in force at any given time.
Board	The Board of Directors of the Company
Company [or "us" or "we"]	Billy Bloggings Ltd.
Companies Acts	Every statute in force at any given time concerning companies insofar as it applies to the Company.

Effective Date	Is the date on which the agreement is signed by all the parties
Group Company	A Company's holding Company and all subsidiaries and all those companies' holding companies and subsidiaries at the Effective Date [using the definitions of "holding Company" and "subsidiaries" as defined in the Companies Acts].
Group	All Group Companies and the Company together.

1.   In the agreement, unless the opposite is clear from the context:

    a.   All singular words include plural ones and vice versa.

    b.   All references to paragraphs, schedules or appendices are to the ones in the Agreement.

    c.   All references to a person include firms, companies, government entities, trusts and partnerships.

    d.   The terms "including" does not exclude anything not listed.

    e.   All references to statutory provisions include any changes to those provisions.

    f.   The headings are not part of the Agreement

2.   This letter of Agreement records the terms on which

you are to serve as a Non-Executive Director of the

Company, starting from [date]. This is a contract for

services and not a contract of employment. You are not

an employee of the Company.

3.   Non-Executive Directors usually serve two three year

terms but may be invited by the Board to serve for

longer. Any term renewal is subject to Board re-

nomination. There is no right to this.

4.   Your appointment is subject at all times to:

a.   The Articles of Association [including any

provisions requiring directors to retire and seek

re-election at any Annual General Meeting.]

b.   Satisfactory performance and any requirement at any time for shareholder approval that the Board considers to be necessary in respect of your appointment or its terms, and

c.   The provisions of applicable law, including the Companies Acts.

5.   Your appointment on the terms of this letter will continue until ended by either party giving one month prior written notice to the other party. We can choose to end this appointment without letting the notice period run its course by making a payment equal to the fees that would have been due during the unexpired notice period, less tax and national insurance contributions and other deductions as required by law.

6.   You will be entitled to payment for your services as a Non-Executive Director at the rate of £XXXX p.a. accruing daily and payable monthly in arrears, less deductions of tax and national insurance contributions. You will not participate in any bonus schemes or in any other benefit in kind arrangements nor will you be entitled to any compensation for loss of office.

7.   The Board may ask you, in its absolute discretion, to become Chairman of the Board or a member of the Audit or Remuneration Committees and you may agree to do so. In such circumstances, you are expected to attend meetings of those committees at a fee to be agreed between us. If you become a member of the Remuneration Committee, you must not hold directorships in the same companies as any of our

Executive Directors, without prior approval of the Board.

8. You must devote such time as is necessary to the performance of your duties as a Non-Executive Director. You confirm by signing this letter that you able to make sufficient time to carry out your duties effectively under this Agreement and that you will advise [name of Company Officer] before accepting other commitments which may interfere with the time spent on your duties under this Agreement.

9. You must attend periodic Board Meetings [normally XX a year], any General Meetings of the Company and, if we ask, meetings of the Audit and/or Remuneration Committees [or any other Committees that you

appointed to] unless you are too ill to attend or your

absence has been otherwise excused. You must spend

enough time preparing for those meetings beforehand.

Non-Executive Directors must work with and through

the Board; they are not expected to undertake

executive duties or to assume executive

responsibilities. We anticipate an overall time

commitment of XXX days a year but this is a non-

binding estimate and does not include the induction

phase or any additional time needed if you are

appointed to any Committees of the Board. You will be

notified of any expected increase in time commitment

on being asked to carry out any additional

responsibilities.

10. You agree to an induction phase to your appointment, where you will make site visits and meet with various levels of our management, auditors and possibly our shareholders. We do not envisage that this will take longer than XX days in addition to your other time commitments.

11. You confirm that by accepting this appointment or performing any of your duties for us, you will not be in breach of any agreement or any other obligations binding on you.

12. Your appointment and this letter of agreement will end immediately without any entitlement to compensation [apart for any unpaid fees accrued up to the date of termination] if:

a.   You are removed as a Director by a resolution duly passed at a General Meeting or otherwise as permitted by law.

b.   You stop being a Director because of any provision of the Articles of Association or because your appointment [or any renewal of your appointment] is not approved by our shareholders where this is a requirement of the Articles of Association or because of any legal requirement including the various Companies Acts.

c.   You become bankrupt or enter into any arrangement with or for the benefit of your creditors including a voluntary arrangement under the Insolvency Acts.

d.   You are now or at any time in the future prohibited by law from being a Director, or

e.   The company ends your appointment in circumstances where [1] you are guilty of any misconduct or have committed any serious or persistent breach of any of your obligations to us or any Group Company; [2] you are found guilty of any fraud or dishonesty; or [3] you commit a criminal offence or are otherwise guilty of any conduct which the Board reasonably believes may danger your or our reputation or the reputation of any Group Company.

13.   If we formally ask you to resign as a Director of the Company or any Group Companies when this Letter of

Agreement or your appointment terminates, however that happens, then you must do this immediately.

14. As a Non-Executive Director, you are part of the Board and must comply with the duties that all Directors owe. You must perform your duties faithfully, effectively and diligently to the best of your abilities and in line with seniority of the role you hold, your knowledge, skills and expertise.

15. In your role as a Non-Executive Director, you must:

a. Help develop and constructively challenge proposals on strategy

b. Scrutinise the performance of our management team in meeting agreed goals and objectives and monitor the reporting of performance.

c. Satisfy yourself on the integrity of financial information and the financial controls and systems of risk management are robust and defensible.

d. Determine appropriate levels of pay of executive directors and have a prime role in appointing and, where necessary, removing executive directors, as well as consider issues of succession planning.

e. Devote time to developing and refreshing your knowledge and skills, including training sessions the Board reasonably recommend for you.

f. Set and uphold high standards of integrity and ethics and support the other Directors in instilling the appropriate culture, values and behaviours within and outside the boardroom.

g. Insist on receiving high quality information sufficiently in advance of Board Meetings.

h. Take into account the views of Shareholders and other stakeholders where appropriate and encourage other members of the Board to do so.

i. Comply with our policies and procedures applicable to Directors that are notified to you.

j. Disclose any direct or indirect interest you may have in any matter being considered at a Board or committee meeting so that it can be decided whether you are permitted to vote under the articles or whether you will not be able to vote because of a direct or indirect conflict of interest.

k. Immediately report your own wrongdoing or the wrongdoing or proposed wrongdoing of any employee or other Director of the Company of which you become aware to XXXX [name of individual] at the Company.

l. Not to do anything that would cause you to be disqualified from acting as a Director.

16. You must exercise your powers in your role as a Non-Executive Director consistent with applicable law, regulations and the Companies Acts. You must behave in the way that you consider, in good faith, is most likely to promote the Company's success for the benefit of Shareholders as a whole, and by law must have regard to [amongst other matters] the:

a.   Likely consequences of any decision in the long run.

b.   Interests of the Company's employees.

c.   Need to foster our business relationships with suppliers, customers and interested third parties.

d.   Impact of our operations on the community and the environment.

e.   Desirability of us maintaining a reputation for high standards of business conduct, and

f.   Need to act fairly as between our Shareholders.

17.   If you are unclear about any of the terms of this Agreement, including your duties and what is expected of you, or you have any concerns, you should contact XXXX [name of individual] at the Company.   If your

concerns cannot be dealt with to your satisfaction or for any other reason you choose to resign, you must write to XXXX [name of individual] at the Company so that this can be reported to the Board.

18.   As soon as your appointment ends, however that happens, or earlier if we request it, you must:

a.   Return to us, all property that you have or control, that belongs to us or relates to our business, including but not limited to all documents and any car, keys, swipe cards, laptops and mobile phones.

b.   Notify us of all passwords used by you on our computer and communication systems.

c.   Delete any such property and information from any electronic devices which belong to you.

19. We will reimburse you for reasonable travel, hotel and other expenses that you incur in performing your duties properly under this Agreement, as long as you comply with any expenses policy in force at the time,

20. We will arrange Directors' and Officers' liability insurance for your benefit. Your participation in that insurance is subject always to the policy terms, conditions and limitations, a copy of which can be obtained from XXXX [name of individual] at the Company.

21. During your appointment, you may work for or be involved in any other business or undertaking as long as:

a. You disclose significant interest to the Board at the start of this Agreement and whenever your interests change during this Agreement.

b. Your outside interests do not create a conflict or potential conflict, or interfere with your duties for us, and

c. The other business or undertaking does not directly compete with the Company.

Nothing in the Letter of Agreement prevents you from holding an investment by way of shares or other securities of or not more than 5% of the total issued share capital of any company listed or dealt in on a recognised stock exchange.

22. During your appointment, you may have access to confidential information concerning us and our

business as well as Group Companies and their businesses, which will be deemed to include any non-public information concerning our or any Group Company's;

a. Finances, operational models, business plans and sales and marketing information, plans and strategies, business transactions, research activities and dealings and affairs;

b. Customers, suppliers, licensors, licensees, agents, distributors or contractors including, without limitation, lists of, identities of, contact details of and requirements of such persons, pricing or price structures, discounts, special prices or special contract terms offered to or by or agreed with such persons;

c.   Existing and planned goods and services and their components and any underlying technology or proprietary materials and/or product lines;

d.   Computer and communication systems, source codes and software.

In each case, whether past, current, future or prospective but not including any information which is or becomes generally available to the public other than through your breach of this Agreement.

23.   You are entitled to request any information about our affairs, which are relevant and reasonably necessary in order for you to fulfil your role under this Agreement.

24. During and after your appointment you must securely store our confidential information and not use or disclose or allow anyone else to use or disclose any of our confidential information, except:

a. As necessary to properly perform your duties for us.

b. With our consent.

c. As required by law or ordered by a Court that has jurisdiction, or

d. To make a protected disclosure within the meaning of section 63A of the Employment Rights Act 1996.

25. You will comply with all lawful and reasonable directions of the Board and with all our rules and regulations. You must not enter into any commitment

on the Company's behalf unless specifically authorised

by the Board to do so.

26.   We may hold and process a wide variety of personal

data about you, including references, personal records,

emails containing personal details, addresses and

details of contractual benefits. Some of this data may

be "sensitive personal data" including information

about:

a.   Your racial or ethnic origin or religious or similar

information in order to monitor compliance

with equal opportunities legislation;

b.   Your physical or mental health to monitor sick

leave and to decide whether you are fit to

perform your duties;

c.   Any criminal proceedings in which you have been involved for insurance purposes and to comply with legal requirements and third party obligations.

27.   We may periodically need to make your records available to Group Companies, professional advisers, governmental and regulatory authorities, including HMRC and other parties which provide products or services to us.

28.   By signing this Letter of Agreement, you consent to us processing your personal data and sensitive personal data and the transfer of that data to any Group Company and our business contacts outside the UK.

29.   You waive all moral rights under the Copyrights, Designs and Patents Acts 1988 [and all similar rights in other jurisdictions] which you have or will have in any existing or future works prepared by you in the provision of your services to us and will not start or support any claims that any use of the works infringes your moral rights.

30.   This Agreement contains the whole Agreement between us relating to the subject matter and supersedes all prior discussions, arrangements or agreements that might have taken place in relation to the Agreement. You agree that you have no remedy for any representations not contained in the letter and you have no claim for innocent or negligent misrepresentation. Nothing in this clause limits or

excludes any liability for fraud or fraudulent misrepresentation.

31. No party may assign, transfer, sub-contract or otherwise make over to any third party the benefit and/or the burden of this Agreement without the prior written consent [not to be unreasonably withheld] of the other party.

32. No variation of the Agreement will be valid or binding unless it is recorded in writing and signed by or on behalf of both parties.

33. The Contracts [Rights of Third Parties] Act 1999 does not apply to this Agreement and no third party has any

right to enforce or rely on any provisions of this Agreement.

34. Unless otherwise agreed, no delay, act or omission by a party in exercising any right or remedy will be deemed a waiver of that, or any other, right or remedy.

35. A provision which by its intent or terms is meant to survive the termination of this Agreement will do so.

36. If any Court or competent authority finds that any provision [or part] of this Agreement is invalid, illegal or unenforceable, that provision or part provision will, to the extent required, be deemed to be deleted, and the validity and enforceability of the other provisions of this Agreement will not be affected.

37. Unless specifically provided by the Parties, nothing in this Agreement will establish any partnership or joint venture between the Parties, or mean that one Party becomes the agent of the other Party, nor does this Agreement authorise any Party to enter into any commitments for or on behalf of the other Party.

38. Other than dealings in the normal course of business, any notice, request, demand or other communication [collectively Notices] to be given under this Agreement will be deemed to be duly given by either party, if;

a. Sent by first class post addressed to the other Party or [in the case of Notice to the Company] its registered office or [in the case of Notice to you] the address that you have last notified to us, or

b.   Given personally to [in the case of Notice to the Company] another Director of the Company or [in the case of Notice to you] to you personally, or

c.   Sent by electronic mail to the business email address of XXXX [name of individual] at the Company or your email address as notified in writing to the Company from time to time.

39.   Any such Notice will be deemed to have been given;

a.   If sent by first class post, 48 hours [or, if sent to or from outside the UK, seven days] after the time of posting and, in proving service, it will be sufficient to prove that the envelope containing such Notice was properly addressed, stamped and put in the post;

b.   If sent by electronic mail, 24 hours after sending.

40.   This Agreement will be governed by and interpreted by English law and claims arising under this Agreement [including non contractual disputes or claims] will be subject to the exclusive jurisdiction of the English Courts.

41.   This Agreement is delivered as a deed on the Effective Date.

42.   Kindly confirm your agreement to the terms set out above by signing the counterpart copy of this letter and returning the copy to XXXX [name of individual] at the Company.

Executed as a Deed by

....

Joe Blow

In the presence of:

....

Witness signature

Name   of   Witness;

....

Address;

....

....

Occupation; ....

Date; ....

Executed as a Deed by Billy Bloggings Ltd.

....

XXXX, duly authorised officer acting for and on behalf of Billy Bloggings Ltd.

In the presence of:

....

Witness signature

Name   of   Witness;

....

Address;

....

....

Occupation; ....

Date; ....

ABOUT THE AUTHOR

Ray Fox

Ray Fox originally qualified with a B.Sc. (Hons.) degree in Behavioural Science (specialising in Industrial Psychology and Human Behaviour) from the University of Aston in Birmingham.

After graduation, he studied for and completed the examinations for The Institute of Chartered Secretaries and Administrators. He is a Fellow of the Institute (FCIS). Following that, he studied for and obtained a Diploma in Company Law and a Diploma in Company Secretarial Practice from the School of Accountancy and Business Studies.

For eight and a half years [from 1979 until 1987], Ray was the Company Secretary of a £50m turnover engineering company. In 1987 he joined Dun & Bradstreet, a US$3B turnover company, as their UK Company Secretary. Over the subsequent seven years, he was promoted to Company Secretary of D & B Europe, then the D & B Group and was subsequently appointed as their UK Director of Legal and Pensions Services. He was also Company Secretary of D & B Group's Pension Plan responsible for all administration and £100M of Pension Fund investments. Ray left D & B in 1994 to set up his own Consulting Practice.

For over twenty years, he has been running a very successful marketing consultancy specialising in the Legal profession generate more Commercial Clients.

Ray is the Founder and Principal of The Bottom Line Consultancy. His Company specialises in providing a full range of support and marketing services to Solicitors and their Practices. Having worked for over 780 different Solicitors Practices, they are probably one of the largest consultancies that specialises in the legal profession. He can be contacted on 01494 483728 or by email at raymondafox@aim.com.

In addition to the above, he is one of the Founder Members and a Director of Core Legal, [see www.CoreLegal.net] which is a networking organisation of professional companies all of whom provide specialist support to the legal profession. He was also a General Commissioner of Taxes and one of the Co-Authors of "Running a Successful Law Firm – Strategies and Tips for Success".

He is active in Freemasonry, having been Worshipful Master of a number of Lodges and is also a member of The Worshipful Company of Chartered Secretaries and Administrators, one of the modern Livery Companies of the City of London.

Ray is also the brains behind a number of highly successful web sites:

www.BottomLineConsultancy.com

www.SolicitorSupermarket.biz

www.RecruitmentForSolicitors.co.uk

www.NEDexchange.co.uk

www.ProfessionalDirectors.co.uk

www.YourEnglishOffice.com

www.YourAmericanOffice.biz

www.TradeAndFinanceDiploma.com

www.StopTheTaxMan.com

www.WorldMoneyExchange.co.uk

www.Estelle-Alan-Group.com

www.EstelleAlanPublications.com

www.CompanyFormationCorporation.com

www.InsuranceForSolicitors.co.uk

www.UKTradeAdvisoryServices.com

www.YourOffshoreBankAccount.biz

OTHER BOOKS BY THE AUTHOR

More Commercial Clients And How To Get Them

A 'How To' Book for Solicitors' Practices
Published: 2014
ISBN: 978-1505488715

I know we don't want to admit it or say the words out loud but here goes – "Generally, Solicitors are crap at marketing". There, I've said it. We all know it's true but what can we do about it? A lot of Solicitors' Practices will spend a lot of money on marketing, but this doesn't often pick up more commercial clients - a group who are often more profitable than a typical private client. This book is about how to get more commercial clients.

How To Make £1,000 Per Week Running Your Own Import / Export Agency
Published: 2015
ISBN: 978-1507722176

Have you ever thought about running your own import / export business? Do you want to know what to do and how to go about it? This handy little book contains tips, the steps, letter and agency contract templates, which you can amend and use for your own purpose. It is absolutely possible to make £1,000 Per Week Running Your Own Import / Export Agency from home.

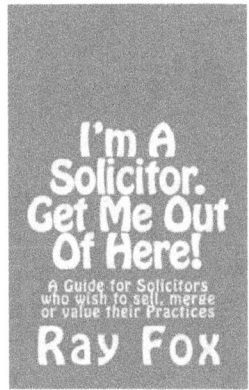

I'm a Solicitor. Get me out of here!
Published: 2015
ISBN: 978-1516950546

Have you thought about where your Practice will be in 12 months, in 3 years, in 5 years time? What plans do you have in case you become ill and are unable to continue working? Do you have Solicitors within your firm who are thinking of leaving because they haven't been offered Salaried Partnership? Likewise, do you have Salaried Partners within your firm who are thinking of leaving because they haven't been offered Equity? What would happen if one of your key fee earners became ill or left? If you are thinking of buying, selling merging or having your firm valued - this book is essential reading material.

How to Make £25-£100k in your Own Venture Capital Business
Published: 2015
ISBN: 978-1514624883

Have you got a burning desire to start your own business? Are you uncertain as to the type of business that you should start? Serial entrepreneur, Ray Fox outlines how you can start your own venture capital business, based from home and make £25,000 to £100,000 per annum.

How To Make £1,000 Per Week Running Your Own Unique Marketing Business
Published: 2015
ISBN: 978-1511693912

Would you like to operate and grow a business working from home? This book explains how you can start your own unique marketing business - working from home, and make up to £1,000 per week doing so.

An introduction to Freemasonry
Published: 2016
ISBN: 978-1533439062

Have you ever wondered about freemasonry? How you can join this 'secret society'? What does it cost to join? What goes on at the meetings? Who are the members? Is it something to do with the occult? or

An Introduction To Freemasonry
Raymond Fox

the illuminati?! **In this book** Lodge Master Mr Fox, explains the background to freemasonry with a focus on the England, UK lodges. This book delves into the history of masonry, what goes on at meetings, how you can join, the festive board, the lodge of instruction, what is expected of you as a mason and more.

OTHER BOOKS WHICH MIGHT BE OF INTEREST

Running A Successful Law Firm
Strategies & Tips for Success
Published: 2014
ISBN: 978-1492870890

Corelegal specialise in working with solicitors / lawyers. Between the contributing authors there is over 100 years collective experience. This book aims to bring that knowledge to you – giving you fresh ideas and perspective. Avoid the expensive, painful and time consuming mistakes that most solicitors make and make your law firm a profitable success!

79 Marketing Ideas For Solicitors

First Published: 2014
ISBN: 978-1505487329

Solicitors are highly qualified individuals who went to law school – and know the law inside out, but yet may have had little / training as to how to actually market and promote what they actually do. Do not be the best kept secret! If you are a sole practice solicitor or are working with law firms in their marketing department this book will give you 79, very doable, very applicable ideas to market the law firm and get potential customers beating a pathway to your door. Some ideas are free, some are easier than others – but one thing is for sure – they all work!

Make The Most of Your Money
How to budget, save and manage your finances.
First Published: 2013
ISBN: 978-1481990639

This book looks at how to make the most of your money. Often the harder you work, the less you have to show for it. This book covers the issue of money. All the stuff you should have been taught in school including income, stocks, bonds, assets, reducing debt, mortgages, loans.

How To Write A Book In Two Weeks (or Less)

First Published: 2013
ISBN: 978-1492273554

Do you have a burning desire to write a book, but don't know how? Have you been thinking about writing a book for a while, but have just never 'gotten round to it?' Would you like to get your book completed quickly? Serial entrepreneur & author Lisa Newton explains how to write a book in two weeks (or less), which works particularly well for writing non-fiction books, business books and self-help books.

Think And Grow Rich
First Published: 2015
ISBN: 978-1505889352

Originally published in 1937, Napoleon Hill interviewed over 500 of the most affluent men and women of his time, and documented their secrets to wealth. Fast forward to present day and business people, top achievers and entrepreneurs alike still refer to this timeless classic. The money-making instructions that Hill outlines are just as powerful today as they were when first written. This exciting updated and revised edition by serial author and entrepreneur Lisa Newton expands on Hill's work and can be used as a workbook.

Constant Cashflow
How to Make Money Flow To You Every Single Day
Published: 2014
ISBN: 978-1 500601225

The problem with 'Cashflow' is that often businesses and individuals are too reliant on just one income stream/ source. Instead of just having 'one/two' jobs or key clients, and 'twenty' expenses, why not turn this around? What this book promotes is that everyday should be a payday - and it explains how and why.

To order further copies of this book please fill in the form:

No. of copies	Title	Price	Total
	More Commercial Clients And How To Get Them	£12.50	
	How To Make £1,000 Per Week Running Your Own Import / Export Agency	£10.00	
	How To Make £1000 Per Week Running Your Own Unique Marketing Business	£10.00	
	How To Make £25k-£100k In Your Own Venture Capital Business	£10.00	
	I'm A Solicitor. Get Me Out Of Here!	£13.77	
	An Introduction To Freemasonry	£8.77	
	Non-Executive Directors	£10.00	
	For P&P add £2.50 for the first book, £1 for each extra book		
	GRAND TOTAL		£

Name: _____

Address: _____

City: _____ Country: _____

Postcode / Zip: _____ Tel. No./Email: _____

I enclose a Cheque made payable to **The Bottom Line Consultancy** for £ _____

Please return forms to: (Photocopies acceptable)
Direct Mail Dept., The Bottom Line Consultancy, Hurst Cottage, Bottle Square Lane, Radnage, Buckinghamshire. HP14 4DP, UK
Enquiries to: fox@estelle-alan.com

The Bottomline Consultancy (directly or via its agents) may mail, email or phone you about promotions or products. [ ] Tick box if you do not want these from us
www.BottomLineConsultancy.com

www.ingramcontent.com/pod-product-compliance
Lightning Source LLC
Chambersburg PA
CBHW071206220526
45468CB00002B/510